Praise for **Ripening.** . .

"Made from the plump and ruddy fruits of her own life, Cari Griffo's *Ripening* is a very rich literary liqueur. These are poems to savor and, like good brandy-wine, will get you memorably drunk. Rare in a first book . . . these are poems with many layers."

Michael W. Eliseuson
Writer and founder of *The Inkslinger's Review*

"Here is a voice as fresh and lifegiving as spring rain. Cari Griffo's poems are ardent and clear-eyed, buoyed by a wry humor that celebrates equally the form of ripening and decline. A lovely debut."

Morgan Farley
Poet and author of *Name Yourself Feast*

"Strong and intricate work by a genuine maker."

Thomas Fitzsimmons
Poet and author of *The Poetry and Poetics of Ancient Japan*

Ripening

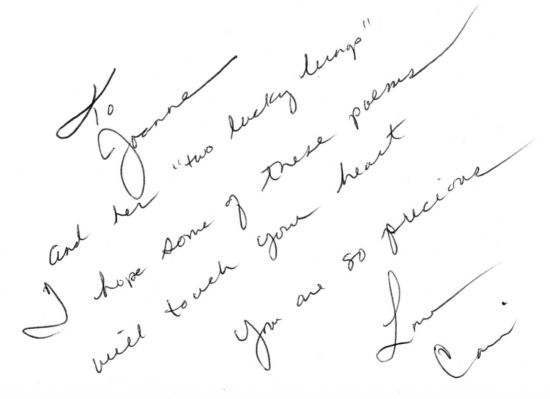

To
Joanne
and her "two lucky lungs"
I hope some of these poems
will touch your heart
You are so precious
love
Con.

Ripening

Cari Griffo

Molti Frutti
productions

Santa Fe, New Mexico

Published by: **Molti Frutti Productions**
1704-B Llano Street, Suite 121
Santa Fe, NM 87505

Edited by Ellen Kleiner
Book design by Richard Harris
Interior art by Karla Winterowd
Cover art by Tal Ronnen
Back cover photograph by Jennifer Esperanza
Cover design by Janice St. Marie

Printed in the United States of America

Publisher's Cataloging-in-Publication Data

Griffo, Cari.
      Ripening / by Cari Griffo
      p. cm.
      Includes bibliographical references.
      ISBN 0-9656981-9-X

      1. Title.
      PS3557.R5446R5646 1997   811'.54
                                 QBI97-40362

10 9 8 7 6 5 4 3 2 1

For my grandparents—
Nana
Nono
Grandpa Rabin
Nanny

Their expressive voices of love,
wisdom, and pride speak their truths.

In Gratitude

My first thoughts of appreciation extend back over the years to my family and friends who took the time to hear me read my poetry—usually on the phone, preceded by "Do you have a minute? This is a short one." Thank you for your continuing encouragement. Thanks also to Frank, who built my first stage. I would like to embrace each audience participant for supporting my performances. The team of Blessingway truly guided my vision of *Ripening:* Ellen Kleiner, for whom I am truly blessed, Richard Harris, and Janice St. Marie. Tal Ronnen, my cousin, I am so appreciative of your talent. Karla Winterowd and Jennifer Esperanza, *Grazie.*

I am grateful, too, for the earlier debuts of the following poems: "Introduced in winter . . . ," *Written with a Spoon: A Poet's Cookbook* (Sherman Asher Publishing, 1996); "Rain in a drought. . . ,' *THE Magazine* (June 1997); "In a Fog," poetry video for the television documentary *The Santa Fe Songworks Series* (1996); "True Love," KSFR 90.7 FM (1996); "Crows in the News," *The Santa Fe Songworks Series* (1996); "Perfect Views," KSFR (1996); "Human in Mountain Time," *Creative Writer's Project* (Summer 1995); "Lucky Lungs," KSFR (1996); "Shopping," *Creative Writer's Project* (Spring 1995); "User," published as a poster in *Inkslinger's Review of New Mexico Books and Authors*, vol. 1, no. 4 (1993).

Contents

The Picking of Fruit

Introduced in winter . . .   13

During the Vulnerable Stage   14

Rain in a drought . . .   15

Rain on the East Coast   16

Pursuing the Heart   18

Tweezing   20

In a Fog   21

Waiting   22

At the Pediatrician's Office   23

Grandpa Rabin Haiku   24

My Vanity Table   26

The Truth of a Friend   27

You Approach the Doorknob   28

On Canvas   30

Morning Walk   31

True Love   32

First Night   34

His First Dinner Alone after Living with Me for Four Months   35

Car Ride   36

Time Is Running Out   37

Crow   40

Crows in the News   41

Person in Need of Listening Skills   42

Moonrise   43

Perfect Views   44

Human in Mountain Time   46

Language Connecting Nothing in Common   48

Losing Blossoms

In the Dental Chair   51

People Are Losing Teeth   53

Saturday Night   55

On Being a Waitress   57

"Lucky Lungs"   60

Lighting the Second-Year Deathday Candle   62

Honey   64

Unbeknownst to Him, He Dreams   65

I am an aquaphobic impostor . . .   67

After a few dates . . .   68

Shopping   70

Inside a Paperweight   72

User   74

Sweet Chariot   75

Inheritance   77

One Day I Never Showed Up Again   78

Greeting Card   80

The Picking of Fruit

Introduced in winter . . .

like spring enters a tree,
cherry blossoms camouflage twigs,
budding earth covers raw dirt,
cotton over lust.
Flesh too soft to hide under goosedown,
we are bare,
        barely enough.
Our souls only sheltered
thicker than the skin of a peach,
thinner than the rind of a watermelon.
As if there were a distance
between fruit and pit,
we prefer to be seeds
craving to be planted.
Apples that grow heavier than stem
dance in the slightest wisp of wind.
Unchoreographed, swaying to touch
ground.
Unpeeled, ripening.
        Crusted sweet juicy pie,
        crusted sweet juicy man,
tasting you in pieces,
delighting in each tiny morsel
sugar could not preserve.

During the Vulnerable Stage

I am a snowflake
in your unfamiliar,
arriving from a coldness
that eludes day as dusk
dimming for the fall of lights.
A speckle of an ice crystal
shimmering in my separateness,
anticipating landing
into the unity of snow,
pristine to the fragility of shape.
I could be like shattered glass,
an unbound shard
scintillating as an unbound flake.
      Flake drawn to tongue
        tinder drawn to flame . . .
I am an ash
in your unfamiliar,
and at the same time,
a callow bird
rising to feathers.

Rain in a drought . . .

in a desert
where people are living
arrives long after the slurp
on a straw suctioning the bottom
of a glass that lavished
a chocolate shake too cold, then creamy
and creamier, rich then richer, when plenty
becomes plastic tapping—long after dirt
is slurped and tapped,
where dust devils itself, evil
could be dependent on a well
and a flower garden on us.
It is our own thirst that waters a pansy bed
which is supposed to die before the threat of fire.
Before we watch it burn, all is burning.

Rain in a drought
in a desert
where people are living
is run into and stood under; thunder
booms are the beat of wells swelling
and pleading for more. When a reservoir wants to be full
it is the cactus, a prickly pear storing drops
to survive off the memory of its feast,
with each cell knowing that it cannot offer itself
for drinking. Water out of a spigot is rain.

Rain on the East Coast

If weather
    permits,
      worms
    shall continue
to till
  soil
today
    blissfully
  in gray
    mist
        and thunder
        pangs
          too painful
        to those starving
     for light
  when lightning
    strikes.
       Pangs
         are too painful,
           malnourished soul
         seizes
           indigo
         of flower,
           craves
            sun-dried
             grass

and bare feet
on firm
ground
crisping
in the brightness
of day.

Pursuing the Heart

Immature thistle,
you have sacrificed flower
to become an artichoke,
gateway to a heart.
The memory of your sweetness
is purchased—you were the roundest
expectant of the largest feast.
As if you cost more than the store was worth,
an asset is found in the most robust dream.

Your preparation is simple,
although some say it is all in the sauce
accentuating the process,
making prickly bract
less tedious.
Eagerly pulled
and dipped,
raised to lower teeth
for the scraping,
a hint of flesh is swallowed
    until it can be chewed,
each leaf becomes flesh
    until flesh is leaf.
In a mossy softness
you are slimming;
purple petals reveal your beat,

enticing the removal of fuzz —
because this time is not virgin,
your choke shall not prevent pleasure
of meat.
This time is succulent
pure sweet.

Tweezing

The first time below the eyebrows
was in Paris, in a youth hostel at 80 Mouttard—
my journal says it was the cheapest
and dirtiest but had a shower and I had my pillow. . .

My traveling companion faces a blurry unframed mirror.
She is barely able to distinguish between a zit
and a beauty mark; with each suave yank
she becomes an unpowdered peaches and cream.
My bleached blonde mustache
seems tacky and revealing as I realize the illusion
of the invisible; the first pull around my lips waters
my eyes but hurts less on the memory of a face with less hair
before the Pill, before the three months of trickery.
In protecting my woman I did not choose to become more of a man.
With each squeeze of the tip, I pull out—fuck the Pill,
fuck the mastery of fake pregnancy; the daily passive ritual
is not a placebo, the will choosing to heal or not to heal. I pull out
and, fuck the Pill, I am a metal bandit on my chin
the way I am a shovel to caliche layer digging for a Manchurian
apricot tree, ramming and pounding a chant for my roommate
who was nearly attacked by a man with an ax. *Stick this ax
right up your ass* (the hole is getting deeper); *stick this ax right up
your ass* (deeper and deeper); *stick this ax right up your ass.* I blister
for the home of roots in a burlap bag; I give them a mansion
so that they may spread to be fibrous, so that with every tweeze
there is the picking of fruit.

In a Fog

My head has known cloudiness—
brocades blunted and dense,
fog unable to rest
    delicately,
like the lace of smoky mist
strewn through limbs of pine
escalating into shadows
toward sky's dwarfing cape,
peaking undiscovered trees
the height of mountain's high.
Hovering sluggish emotions
are the fuzzy of my high,
slow to drift,
waiting for the clearing,
waiting to be charged
by sparks of sun-ray
electricity,
    melting puffs,
    heating trees
    of the highest order
    to rise
    again.

Waiting

I think of all the Judys
and the pink lipstick
applied at five o'clock, attending
to each door creak with a jump
and then a bolt, only to find a swinging screen
is caused by the wind and not the hand
of the man they seem to be alive
for. You spend the entire day
in you, and then for love, dinner burns.
You wouldn't have desired
to eat when it was ready, because
this is the wait of anticipated company,
of what really makes you hungry—
not like the wait after chemo
or unprotected sex. You are waiting
for a dormant ground to brighten,
for the flowering of weeds.
The door chimes a key chain,
yet longing has been too long,
for what could have been a leap
of so-glad-to-see-you is a comforting
rush of relief, a so-glad-you-are-home.

At the Pediatrician's Office

"You're next, honey" is dreadful,
so she continues to read her book
as if every word were pronounceable
without illustrations. This is not next
in a line at the fair, waiting to have her face
painted or her hair strung in ribbons and braided.
She is told it is just a checkup,
but this is where stethoscopes gave her goose bumps
in a humid heat that did not spare air-conditioning
or cotton balls or the smell of rubbing alcohol
and where, at her last visit for a shot, clammy
turned to a hot soaking red and, with stamping feet,
she steamed a hate for everyone.
She could not know that a prick
is not really painful, or that a mannequin
in the store is not really a playmate. When it comes time
to leave her friend, she demands, "*No,* I won't. I am not going.
I won't. *No.*" The nurse had said it hurts
less when you stop crying, to relax your arm;
she did not tell her that someday this will be the stubbornness
that perseverance is made of—a trait of a woman
with standards, steady feet, and a plan
for a new plan.

Grandpa Rabin Haiku

Overcooked salmon
she buys shoes for $800
who cares

Loud truck
he is on velvet over holes
wind over words

Summer rain
money given for piggy bank
and candy

Cloudy Sunday
how is your love life?
phone to ear

Fine dining
aglio e olio and cracked pepper
al dente

Dry humor
you meet his approval
dust on leather

Giant seagulls
a Coney Island merry-go-round
a pink bear

Eye contact
how much money do you make?
they laugh

Stale smell
tokens for subway
fast doors

Cape Vincent
perch on a hook
fish-fry

Starlit night
Pearl on Broadway
he's bored

My Vanity Table

Pressed powder music box
is the scent of Nana
and its gold
the color of her Italy,
the gleaming gift
of a male caller.
Music dribbles
from years of opening
the cover, and now powder puff
is bare and unable to reveal
her makeup
face. I have known her olive
and lines of worry;
she should have clung
to this metal container,
like Miss Havisham
and her bride-cake,
placed in an attic
to store these notes.

The Truth of a Friend
(to Tim)

You flex your armor
like muscles
elongated for the lift,
firm for the stretch,
not too heavy or too far;
without becoming too sore
you bulk to our friendship.
We can't make trouble,
for you make tracks
deep in crunchy snow —
with more fat
than the thinning fat
of antlers trudging
toward brittle twigs.
Prints cannot melt too soon;
hungry for the mud
that claims a season,
you keep walking,
changing
into appropriate
shoes.

You Approach the Doorknob
(to Carla)

I was your father's
wombless lover
and you my papoose,
the unexpected greater fate
unprepared for your dig,
arriving in shards
sacred to its vessel.

Delivered on wings,
six hours soared
past fifteen years.
In a red prom dress
flaunting its flames,
tamed by your baby steps
sparking before too hot,
you did not need to be put out
like the raid of locusts
to crop
or beetle to potato.

You were the carrots
in my cabbage soup
cooked at 3 a.m.;
when your room was empty
my worry had to be busy.

I chopped the ingredients
that Nana said were easy—
foolproof, the flavors blend,
no need to add herbs.
Your arrivals were spicier:
    the drummer was hot
    you danced all night
    you're mad at Sherrie
    Chris needed a ride
    bouncers took your fake ID.
Laughter burst
over B-movie TV
and into the kettle
as if you were daylight
spreading its miles
to the bedroom.
You made me chuckle
silent chuckles
of my wilder nights into dawn.
I wonder if I would have laughed
if someone were listening.

On Canvas

My Aunt Nancy says this ballerina
needs a new frame. Pearled white and 50s
she hung in my mother's childhood
before she was given to mine. In my bedroom
of red, white, and blue, I nightmared snakes
and a playground; I was on top of a tall slide,
and could see them squirming
at the bottom, where dirt was carved
for someone to be waiting. I gripped
the curved rails until my hands smelled
like their metal as I refused to slide down,
but I was pushed, and before my feet touched
the cluster of snakes, I woke to a night-light
and her blue-and-white lace tutu. In fear I stared,
my eyes squinting until she was blurry
and moving. I watched her tie her laces
and point her toe-shoes to dance on pointe.
Outside of the frame she pliéd
on my dresser and my piggy bank. Spinning
and spinning we talked. I told her how beautiful
she was. It wasn't just her grace, but she seemed older
and confident, the way she moved out of the frame;
she became more alive than I felt frozen
in a dream, or Gelsey Kirkland felt frozen
in her prima ballerina life. Unframed, she left her book
Dancing on My Grave lying forever awake.

Morning Walk

I am geared, with or without Willie
my dog, and always with a tight grip
on my Mace spray and a visualization
of my woman invulnerable, alone
and not asking to be raped, looking
confident and strong and ready to beat
the shit out of anyone who tries, shoulders
back, head propped to be slightly stuck-up
in a walk that is smooth and brisk with full
sweeping arm extensions. I am a woman in the arroyo
who would resist, faking my fear
and fearing that a thief of power, in his most silent
moment, visualizes his target—a woman alone
and a perfect bush. In his mind his hand clamps
her voice; she becomes light and draggable (he is inflating),
a Raggedy Ann with an occasional whimper, a slight "no"
or "please"; he thinks she's meek (he is inflating), her fists
are feathers, her nails blunted, there is only one way to enter;
he is inflated. The Olympic diver uses visualization to achieve
his entrance into water: before the bounce he sees the tuck,
the full pike position with arms wrapped around knees-to-chest
for the perfect triple flip that snaps into elongation
from fingertips to toetips as if rigor mortis has set in, into the water
a ripple. A woman walks by with a Walkman muffling
her ears; I ask myself, how will she hear a man sneaking
up behind her? There is a brisk speed walker with her elbows
bent, fisting weights; I wink at her weapons.
Maybe I should be on a bike.

True Love

I want to say, "Good morning, my love"
the way I say, "Cookie,"
with the endearment of thirty years
of knowing the type of my sweet.
Committed to crunch—
cinnamon in Snickerdoodles,
trips to Elite Cookie Shop, smelling
its slogan, "The extra good cookie"—
I will desire this palace until death
do us part. I crave Vanilla Icebox
as much as at fifteen
making them lunch that Soft Molasses
were too soft for,   too quiet.
Adolescents know that chewing
should have an ego,
in a molar moment of Gingersnaps
a siren cannot be heard, Hermits
are full of ingredients without
a presence, Half Moons are half cakes.
Exquisite are the Marble marveled
as Italian imports; Linzer lingers
throughout the day, leaving its seeds
in my grooves; Wedding Cookies shed
powdered tears, and I still crush and pick
their nuts. I can't salivate to Chocolate
Chip—a disguised bitter is too aggressive

in an undiscovered batter. But discovering "no"
at two, "OK" conquers any cookie to taste
good. I temper-tantrumed
for them when both hands
needed to hold the reward;
I lay on the floor
kicking kitchen cupboards,
pleading, "Coooookie, cooooookie."
"Good morning, my love."

First Night

We check into the inn
and are not yet relaxed
at its healing hot springs;
I pay and she gives you the key.
It has been a long August
(your busy season)
and this is our getaway.
A credit card number guaranteed
late arrival as we drove through the dinner
hour of a small town, trying to decide
where to eat, but unable to agree —
and then came the loss of hunger. In our room
we blame each other, the restaurants
we could have tried; then the revealing,
the I-don't-likes, our nonsmokers' eyes burning
in a burnt orange motel room with ashtrays,
sobbing
over the missed mini-encounters
smudged by a busy day. Without dinner
conversation we come to see our us —
we are unwinding like our first sex. The hot
minerals call us in, but first a hug in the icy
midnight air. Sulfur and arsenic tingle
us into a soft dough, kneading out our rough throats.
We sweat out our toxins.

His First Dinner Alone
After Living with Me for Four Months

I take the leftover broccoli
to work for my lunch
and am surprised at how finely
it is cooked, his accompaniment
to hot dogs and Hormel all-beef chili,
as if they were too much of a treat.
He needed a dark green vegetable for absolution
steamed till just tender for fear of mushy florets.
He had his vitamins with cracked pepper
and lemon, the way I like to chew veggies—
still tasting their earth, never creaming spinach
the way his dog is smothered in a bun.
Ah yes, what to eat when she is not home.

Car Ride

Frank says that a dog's
sense of smell is one-quarter of a million
times that of a human's.
Willie, standing on all fours
in the backseat, wishing
this two-door four-by-four
had rear windows that could open,
squeezes her head
between Frank's shoulder and the door
to sniff the outside air.
As we span our heads, she begins smelling
our new views with more excitement
than she shows out in the backyard.

Amid pastures with cows and horses and feeding
troughs, dark mucky ponds, a shell of a house
boarded up with weathered wood, scrub oak
with drying leaves, bales of hay and rusted fencing,
farm equipment left behind, tailings
revealing a copper mountain's past, a sign reads, Hogs
Are Beautiful. The way her head is distended
and bobbing, one would think she'd be radically
appalled by eau de toilette.

Time Is Running Out

When I am old
I will drive fast
spending the least amount
of time in a car
because I will know
that time is moving fast
and the need to be where
I am going is more important
than how I get there.
I will be greedy
like a stockbroker on Wall Street,
hungry as a dog
valuing any trashcan
with an odor
of rancid rot.
I will be counting
my hours of dependence
on an automobile,
hours spent traveling
through nowhere
to take me somewhere—
even to O'Neil's Garage, my church,
where lemons are blasphemy—
praying deeply and desperately:

I need you to start,
I can't afford to miss work,
please don't stall,
I can't be late.
You are my bills,
get me to my job
so I can pay for you.

When I am old I will drive fast,
faster than a newly licensed
teenager with a lead foot
of courage, showing off.
I, with the same courage,
will be tarnished and humble,
but not too humble
to argue a speeding ticket,
asserting that cop cars
should flash snail-pacers.

I am on the expressway
heading to Nana and Nono's
house. The left-hand lane
is no longer for passing;
it is crawling.
Every lane is slowing.
In the congestion
I imagine me as their *bambina*

and their words of *bella e dolce;*
my cheeks are pinched,
occhi di bella.
Completely frustrated
I am nearing
the left-lane culprit;
traffic is loosening
like a blown nose.
I blow my horn
because I know that car.
Nana is pointing her nose
above a tightly gripped wheel;
Nono sits still.
I can't release tension
by blaming senior citizens,
for these are my grandparents —
the entire time it was my grandparents.
I honk again and honk and honk.
Nono stares straight ahead;
he won't look. I want him to look,
to roll down his window
so I can scream,
"Hurry, faster,
you need to be where you are going, faster,
you don't have much time left,
hurry."

Crow

Neck stretches your beak,
pointing the distance
from the tip of your tail, blacker
than a night cave.
You could be in flight cawing
caw
caw,
instead of shimmering slicker
than oil on blacktop
that directs the sun
to extol greasiness.
Landing
is always worth the nibble
nibbling
nibbling.

Crows in the News

They should have been delinquents
or vandals, scoundrels placing
rocks on the railroad tracks
in Japan. Such mischievous behavior
must be human, but spies
find crows derailing trains.
They are known to be smart,
dropping walnuts to be crushed
in front of moving cars,
but NPR says they are not clever
enough to distinguish between rocks
and nuts. I prefer the notion of crows
scenting a cargo full of corn
delivered far from its fields;
the thought of Tippi Hedron
and eyeballs that could be more tempting
than corn on the tracks,
nibbling
nibbling.

Person in Need of Listening Skills

You babble like a brook
without a cadence;
without its rocks
you are not still—crescendo slapping crescendo
you are a wave to shore shouting
high tide—
unlike the brook hushed
in a brisk breeze, harmonized
with the flutter of leaves,
dragonfly's chase to mosquito
buzzes, sweeping in and out of baritone.
You could play in this orchestra.

Moonrise

Ode to mountain lungs
breath without a pulse.
As you take all day to fill
swan glides on water,
clouds drift in sky,
sunflowers rotate.
In one pure inhale
with one clear exhale,
you blow up and out
the full moon.

Moonshine,
brighter than any revelation
and any constellation,
reminding us of our own quest for brilliance,
    of our zest for living.
Beyond our own footpaths,
beyond knowing numb extremities are asleep,
    tonight let them rest,
let them float in this buoyancy.

Ode to the moon,
grand certainty of the earth,
presence demanding a shadow to follow.

Perfect Views

Your house is your castle
on top of a mountain;
where there was once legacy
your purpose is a view.
Kings like Herod the Great
played hard to get: he constructed
thousands of feet above the Dead Sea.
And when Jerusalem was stolen from the Jews
it held a grander destiny—Masada,
a mesa to which zealots escaped for two years,
choosing suicide over submission to the Romans.
And you with your unpaved road, ditches
and rocks to the top in your Range Rover
forever remind you of your bumpy road
to the top,
of what you can afford.
Fooled into paying a high price for beauty
you awed with the people now beneath you
in each sunrise,
through the skyline of piñon, its soft peach-light
dripping into dawn, and in every sunset
the uninterrupted foothills rolling into shadows
that cannot be captured on canvas, the feeling
of something we cannot touch.
When we look up with the insatiable desire of sight
we suspect we have arrived, like settlers

after months of travel through flat land, their destination
a view of a mountain range.
How disarranged this is, with an all-windowed
house blocking the tip of a peak that becomes so ordinary
we can ignore it, pretending to see the rest,
imagining that it must have felt too good
to play on top of snowdrifts, shoving
other kids downward so you could claim, screeching,
"I am king of the mountain."

Human in Mountain Time

How many eyes
have chipped
this rock called erosion?

Piercing mountain
with a distance
that shrinks its hardness
into a soft view
requiring roots
to prevent its wobble.

Many eyes
have chipped
this rock called erosion.

Squinting peaks
into layers
as if a collage
could not reveal
the speck of a human life span.

Eyes have chipped
this rock called erosion.

And how many lips
have convinced words
that they were names
for an unpronounced majesty?

Eyes and lips
have chipped
this rock.

Language Connecting Nothing in Common

How ineffable a word
becomes when meaning
is not in its definition. An artichoke
has choked me and from now on I will prevent
the tightening of my throat,
but who is arti? As Steven Pinker
wonders, why do we park in a driveway
and drive on a parkway, why do we recite
at a play and play at a recital? If you were born
on a cusp, would you truly have a double-sign identity
or are you merely reacting?
A ball rolls down a hill
across a curbed street; it will slow down at the second
curb, jump over it, and stop itself in the grass.
In one feeding, a baleen whale
will eat at least 4,000 pounds of krill,
but when there are clouds
I do not necessarily crave rain.
Rather, the overcast tempts me
to breathe in slowly and deeply through one nostril
while alternating to the other for exhale.

Losing Blossoms

In the Dental Chair

You say you haven't heard George Winston
in a while, so I offer you headphones
but this reminds you of your brother—
he died one year ago, he used to play piano.
You would rather not listen to music
at all but it is too late, your tears
have arrived—not because of the usual dentalphobia
that keeps people away for years, only to experience
more pain than the sadistic dentist
could ever have caused, the pain that's finally brought
them back, the bleeding gums, the rancid odor,
the sharp point on their molar, the inability to chew
on one side blocked out for too long.
It has been a long year that you have been sorrowing
and it would be comforting to be in water, in the ocean;
you say you feel safe there and I can see your eyes
belonging there, immersed wide open in a vast swirling
sea drinking your salt drops. A dolphin whistles,
you laugh
at the possible reasons for my aquaphobia:
     I was five months old and my Nanny
     was bathing me in the kitchen sink with the television
     on; a newscaster broke through her soap opera
     to announce that President Kennedy had been shot
     and killed. Her hands released me to cover
     her mouth turning to the set in disbelief;

when she remembered me she grabbed
me from the bottom of stainless steel.
My Nana watched half her senior class drown
in an undertow at Crystal Beach;
from shore she watched my childhood
that way, my sisters and I in the water amid her terror
and distrust, her *"Mama mia, mama mia,"*
and "Joey, watch them. *Dio mio, dio mio."*
You notice tears welding to sockets, drying
the way you dry in the sun, the salt crusted
into your skin; you rest in the sand still undulating,
feet sifting and molding warm granules
into the perfect coddle like a foot entering a slipper
of brand new lamb's wool. The curl of a wave's lip
swishes foam to land, darkening its place of retrieval
to be frothed over again, spreading further into completion,
into a rippling that is as quiet as a spider spinning a web.
You rise for another plunge.

People Are Losing Teeth

(in commemoration)

Eight hundred dollars for a root canal
treatment, and I know how much files
cost and the price of reamers.
You want to save my tooth's nerve —
what nerve of yours does not take payments?
You believed in them for student loans
or your house, but you are too injected
with income, as if it were Novocain
opening your bills and writing out checks.
While you buy your children's
school clothes, someone is trying
to afford school lunch; someone like you is filling
fillings while others' jaws are aching
because they couldn't stop the rot
that would have prevented eight hundred
dollars for a specialist,
an endodontist who is an egodontist
serving as a pawn
in a health-care system, with a care
that is not concerned if it is a luxury
for people to keep their teeth.
Why should we have to buy back
what we were born with? Purchasing a porcelain
crown is not the same as buying
a crown of pearls to be visited in a safe-deposit box;

when people are told that extraction is an option
they are not choosing
leather upholstery
or a tile backsplash.
They need to be told that only one set of teeth
must absolutely be given up—when we made money from
fairies, taking out the trash,
or cleaning our rooms.
We should have been told that in the real
world you don't make the bucks
by losing your teeth to the pillow,
that someday you'll be paying
to save your bite.

Saturday Night

Telephone chirps like a birdcall
    revealing its kind,
    night wings of flock leader
    guiding me into flight.
Calling the wrong number,
    ringing the wrong person.
    I want to make it right
      and call an old lover.
    I want to play Joan Baez
      and hear "Diamonds and Rust."
    I want to get drunk
      and know booze in the morning,
      convince my body it's loved,
      convince myself to believe
      in Saturday night.
Evening ritual of consistent lover
    performance holiness could not bless,
    yet I was blessed with devotion,
    breeder of true experience,
    denier of faith.
Grief is an unrighteous follower.
    Counting the men past the fingers on my hands,
    tonight I desire to count the men
    past the fingers on my hands
    plus the toes on my feet.
Grief is an unrighteous follower —

a woodpecker without a tree,
a leech without blood.
Craving to be fed,
    you licked your ice cream too fast.
    How can a frozen tongue taste the sweet?
    After many licks,
    cold swells loneliness
    a honeymoon cannot melt,
    until in my alone,
    I am Mocha Fudge Swirl.

On Being a Waitress

I needed The Spring House
and the short little gold
jumper with a ruffled
apron, that could have been shorter,
    but I wanted to try it without props,
the way I was trying my first
apartment and my neighbor
The Fortune Garden. You studied
your books as I studied
the frequency of roaches
that were supposed to belong
in the kitchen of chefs; a man returned
his salad because it was crawling.
A pair of shoes waited
by the side of my bed—
it was better for wood heels
to do the crunching
than the skin of my feet.

Roaches rattled out of greasy
fans, coffee rattled
onto white blouses;
I hurried but was too slow
for people to know
that they were paying.

You liked my brown eye shadow—
it was dark
for the twelve businessmen
on their expense account dinner,
indulging in martinis, with a "Hey, cutie,"
and then lightly leaving an enormous tip
that felt like an entrance
fee for their scanning and viewing.

Demoted to cocktail lounge . . .
    you said you loved
me, but the drunks pinched
my rear end that you made sore,
that a Saturday night couldn't save.
Standing on stage, you made love
to your bass the way you made love
to your books. Saturday night
needed me in the private party
room
        carrying peas upstairs
        on a tray, like cocktails flat
        on my palm. Above my shoulder
        are peas for one hundred,
        each step up heavier
        from the weight of the platters,

not the peas; practice without platters
crashes the ceramic, not the peas—
they are rolling, bouncing
down steps, away from mouths
of one hundred. Hundreds of peas
splatter without warning; bus boys
slip with their trays clattering,
smushing peas like smushing roaches
and pinches, peas stomped and
squashed,
stomping you off the stage
squashed into the stairs
with peas and roaches.

"Lucky Lungs"

This is what they named her fund-raiser.
She has cystic fibrosis and needs new lungs;
those who cannot attend can send a donation,
which means all I have to do is write a check.
Yet I am writing this poem way before that,
every day I know it.
All I need to do is write a check.

I am at the grocery store buying shrimp,
I give my OK to a little over a pound
rationalizing the ice, and I remember
that I haven't sent money; the price of seafood
makes the taste of it so predictable.
How much do I pay for her transplant?
For two lungs, any amount seems too little.

I hope she knows a lot of people
and then it occurs to me that it is people
she needs to pay. I hand my money to the cashier,
one hundred thirty dollars, cash dollars
for sweaters and slippers that could have been a check
for her lungs; instead, acrylic makes me believe I'll prevent
a cold this winter. What could she have prevented?
She was never expected to live this long, to become
this woman. A woman in Iran is forced to spend an entire
lifetime preventing her woman and I can't send funds
to her.
All I need to do is write a check.

It seemed easier to pick out flowers for my sick
grandfather, to have them sent, to visit my brother-in-law
in the hospital when he shot a nail with a nail-gun
through his tibia, a nail that just needed to be pulled out.
I have responded to depressing phone calls better
than this—the pleading not to do it, the convincing
that suicide is not an alternative—and now I want to play
those conversations over again, ask them, "How are your organs?"
tell them they are lucky to have two healthy lungs,
call them "Lucky Lungs" . . . with that they could live.

Lighting the Second-Year Deathday Candle

This is the growl
of my Nanny, who could make a pit bull whimper
and will never die; the way found bones survive
I have discovered her dentures; the acrylic stubs
of stain were the verve of her curled lips,
clicking as if she had a secret or deserved
a clapping.

This is the growl
of June Smith, who hated her name and never forgave
her last ex for making it too common
to find in the phone book, and her mother for naming
her after a month she wasn't born in, to make
sense of December when nothing blooms
except a mood of the Great Lakes in a great
winter and a cold that is felt before the shiver
of a never-ending season, when dormancy is the fear
of your own breath; there is no way to know June
before a tulip. And then, like a well-watered
crab apple tree, she perked into her queen
ruling all creditors of credit cards,
filling her car with more toys than I at eight
could fit under my bed. In her hospital bed
she tried to tell me that she should have loved
more and that the worst part was having no focal
points, always going around in circles, around
and around.

This is the growl
of June, who sat on a couch that remained indented
long after her skinny body lifted from the cushion,
shaking her lighter to her cigarette
as if it were her finger to her father
or to her inherited genes; on the hottest
days she was a drought caught smoking,
spreading throughout the neighborhood to Gelatos
not for the ice cream but to sit in front on a bench
to be a character in the shade, famous to yuppies
who lived in Victorian houses with ornate
trim on the outside. She could cut through the pile
of anyone's junk mail to reveal their certified
letters.

This is the growl
of my Nanny, who always wanted to be admired
and was never too delicate to give a hug full of desire
like the desire that swallows a pill without water;
we smudged the mascara crumbs off her face
and neatly applied more to her lashes,
trying to disguise her rattling and hide the baby
behind her rattle rattling her loamy life
stuck in a wave of good-bye that was less feeble
than my telling her, "You are admired," knowing
that she would rise into her white light
without a tremble.

Honey

"Honey?" he asks.
"Honey in your coffee?"
"Honey!" he calls.
If I could melt
into his cup
to make a hot brew,
I would not be sweet.

But it's homemade
by him
and hundreds of bees,
with hundreds of "me"s
sticking in it.

Use me,
bake with me—
your honey
will rise.

Unbeknownst to Him,
He Dreams

Sun streams into the quiet
shadow of your breath,
raising morning to the lids
of a deep sleep
and then to butterfly-kisses.
You say I am lucky to remember
my dreams; tossing and turning
you are my night
crisscrossed in the promise of light.
 Standing still but pacing
 I am about to marry
 my first fiancé.
 A room full of women
 is positive he is God;
 I doubt he is "the one,"
 nothing feels right;
 "Don't you know he is wise?"
 I am hopscotching
 onto dry spots
 of narrow concrete slabs
 deeply immersed in water,
 escaping the speed
 of a power boat
 without a driver,
 its bow in chaos.

People are flailing.
I am its chaser
determined to tackle
the ignition;
my father is bombastic
leading a tuxedo entourage,
his arms fling
like a plastic toy
wobbling on a spring,
*"Jesus Christ, leave
it alone. Jesus Christ."*
Suavely I leap
over slick lacquer
and cut off its power.
Interpreted: you caress the losses
that led me to you, aiming
a good-morning smooch
as if already tilled
for your awakening.

I am an aquaphobic impostor . . .

a hungry current during a high lunar tide
salty and foaming at the cusp of my wave,
all the while knowing that my lifetime is a peak
and then a slap to shore, roaring
what I could have been before my return to Mother:
an undertow, quiet and insidious,
a moral lesson baiting to catch humans
fearing their own beasts while swirling the beast
in me. I hum to them that I can see their birth
the way I have watched eggs and plankton
mingle, coral becoming porous, a barracuda
losing teeth; and when minerals became too dense
for our living in a Dead Sea, it was me, the body of water
still wet, infinitely and portently aging.

After a few dates . . .

I try to smile
    just as I would—
it is of humor,
but your blond hair
is not his silver hue.
Man of my woman,
the muscle of our strength
is like a fox
attaching one to its grace.
    I am floral
drowning in his spice,
drowning in this muse.

While you of Play-Doh
crave to be shaped,
contrived by female
    or anyone,
too eager in defining
"to be,"
prowling yourself
with people of substance
as if it could be stolen.

You are a mold of alginate
fast drying for the impression;
I see me in you until you are transparent.
There is a kindled room,
    champagne tongue hums
        to me,
        with Sade
        and our night.
You press rewind on machine.

Shopping

Three thousand miles away
I did not have to blow breath
into the lines of your face
enough to recognize you standing in a checkout lane
as common as today's date.

I have you nailed to the wall
marking the day of your return,
away from this man you nudged
to make room for your purse
in a cart that moves because of him.
      Because of him
        you are here.

I am a cold vegetarian
in a well-preserving meat department,
puking up our four years
and your years with his years.

I am a mallet
pounding out his past,
tenderizing a moment for me
from his love for you,

or his hate,
or his conveyer-belt feet,

gliding you and the cart onward
past barrels of unweighed candy,
pushing me into a store with teenage friends,
stolen treats unwrapping themselves.
An appalled shopper declared
we should be ashamed
and made certain we were asked to leave.

Politely he assures me
that the peaches are sweet,
but the cart is empty
and I am still helping myself to the bulk.

Inside a Paperweight

How could one have preserved
this skeleton
first found as a dandelion
    alive in a field?

Deceived
by capturing its spine
that gave strength
to this dusty bloom, once
escapable, that in yellow
could have been a mother's
first gift.

So delicate
until a tornado
would not be able to blow
these leftover puffs
hinting seeds,
a dignity under glass
reveals the lack of respect
that tried to grasp
it, only to lose it.

How could one have preserved
this skeleton
    first found alive?

Your florets were the clothes
of your ghost;
despite the power
of sun and rain,
fate could not give
you away
in multitudes.

User

White of this drug
is lucid as snow
that melts upon flesh.

Absorbed as coal
branding pistol to hand
overseer of slaughter.

Slumlord of bruised streets
inhaling their armies,
unacquainted with their bullets.

Sweet Chariot

The wind could have allowed
a winter flu commercial
to film its cure today;
it was a miserable howl.
It was Shirley's memorial service.
Yet the sun was shining,
and to sell medicine
    to nonbelievers,
it must be gloomier.

Even body fat would have known
that the pew was too hard
for my friend's pain,
forcing us behind her back
to see her curls bob
every time she felt her mother.
Baby Shayne conquered all cries
louder than the organ's lisp
of "Sweet Chariot."

The coffee should have tasted
like the smell of straw,
but the grounds were too coarse
for the impostor percolator
      in Shirley's kitchen,
      brewing forty servings,

for fewer people
boozing it up
down in the basement—
their claim to good grief.

Inheritance

I am leeched
onto this bedroom
where dust preserves time
for my aunt,
who never bred adulthood
into the frame of this bed
or this closet
harboring vintage clothes
inevitable to light switch,
packed into a corner
as if they could hide in peeling paint,
and I with an ancient-young heart
could smother its mothballs
to accommodate Nana's postmenopause.

Am I femininity
      reborn
replenishing veins in her breasts?
She wonders what an orgasm
is, bewildered by *The New Our Bodies, Ourselves;*
its thickness leans
against my great-grandfather's mahogany chest,
a labored masterpiece born
flawless for our family
outliving his calluses,
reservoir of sweat.

One Day I Never Showed Up Again

I spent the summer cleaning
for you and pruning
with you; a nurse's aide bathed
your retired doctor-husband
who chirped several good mornings,
his dementia awakening my route to chores
with "How can I help you today?" My vigorous
heart couldn't tell him that I was in a T-shirt and shorts
in his living room.

You liked me to make the bed first
the way you learned in WWII—
the sheets with hospital corners
tucked in at the sides—
hiding what kept you warm
under the bedspread, tightly securing your calves
in case of a nightmare, the kicking of feet, the need to be coddled.

The aide brought her own lunch.
Dishes are clicking and a door seals
itself before it closes; you are setting the dining
room table with three cloth napkins. I think
of how I stood on my bicycle pedals panting
up the early morning traffic-hour
hill and the red lights during a second wind,

my friends telling me to hurry and finish early
(I didn't consider them demanding).
It was too easy not to stay for the stewed rhubarb;
half a sandwich was long enough, even if it was a paid
lunch. And now that I am paying for lunch
I would have eaten two sandwiches on hard rolls
on a day off with an afternoon full of Mason jar rhubarb
to find out what your life was like when your husband
came home at 6:00, or what made you plant
the peony in the backyard.

Greeting Card

A rape crisis advocate
brings to a team meeting
a card seemingly generic
with a forest and animals
in bright colors
that I have never seen in all my hikes;
with every M & M candy
I wonder what inspired the dye.
An advocate is undergoing chemotherapy
and we can all sign if we would like,
and I would like not to be panicked
because I do not know what to say.
I hear a voice telling me to tell the truth:
I am shocked that you have breast cancer,
at this conference table reserved
for survivors of rape
the crisis hotline and the misery
that spirals out of each phone call
are rarely isolated to one incident.
This is when I feel helpless—
wondering how to give enough empathy
to an entire lifetime of abuse, how not to cringe
at the attack of armed lumps,
or your fight for your breasts,
for your life (tell her the truth). I am horrified by
the thought of pesticides and scientists

who trust there are modes
of killing that can discriminate. I am so thankful
my mother is not using hormone replacement,
I wonder if you have eaten too many grapes,
my Nanny smoked too many cigarettes
and died of lung cancer, Shellee's mom died of lung
cancer, never smoked and loved bars;
anything I write hints malignancy.
You are in my prayers
and peace,
Cari.

About the Author

CARI GRIFFO is a poetry event. Performing her work in collaboration with musicians, she radiates exuberance and pure love. She resides in Santa Fe, New Mexico. This is her first book.

Molti Frutti Productions

ORDER FORM

Quantity	Title	Amount
_____	***Ripening*** by Cari Griffo. Book, $12.00 each	_____
_____	***Ripening,*** recited by Cari Griffo. CD containing excerpts from the book, set to music, $14.00 each	_____
	NM sales tax of 6.25% (for New Mexico residents)	_____
	Please add $2.00 per item for shipping and handling; $1.00 per item on orders of two or more	_____
	Total Amount Enclosed	_____

Kindly mail your order, together with your name, address, and check or money order, to:

Molti Frutti Productions
1704-B Llano Street, Suite 121
Santa Fe, NM 87505
505-466-1264
800-598-7302

Thank you for your order. To inquire about a live performance of *Ripening*, please contact Molti Frutti Productions.